YOU CAN BE A HERO

story by
BECKY OLMSTEAD
with Karen George

pictures by
Meagan Bateman
& Camille Paradis

Cataloging-in-Publication Data has been applied for
and may be obtained from the Library of Congress.

ISBN 978-1-7331864-1-4

Copyright © Becky Olmstead

Book design and illustration by Meagan Bateman,
Camille Paradis and Karen George

Published in 2021 by Generation Now

Printed in United States of America

To my two favorite heroes,
♥Isabella & Oakley♥

The world needs who you
were made to be!

XO, Grandma

God made you

uniquely you

and likes you just
the way you are.

---

you have special abilities
and talents that God can
use to change the world
with his **revolutionary
love + power.**

4

THE WORLD NEEDS WHO YOU WERE MADE TO BE.

Are there things in your world that need to change?

You can be a **HERO** and change your world!

HOPE

LOVE

truth!

♥!!

There's a rad revolution of **LOVE** beginning.

freedom!

think BIG!

7

It's made up of kids who want to do something important.

LOVE IS

ON ITS WAY

HEY!
YOU'RE HERO
MATERIAL!

Heroes spread the message that people can come out of the darkness and into the light of **GOD'S LOVE.**

Have you ever wondered
if God is real?

you can SEE GOD, 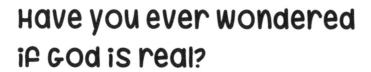 just look!

God's reflected in all
that he's created.

you can reflect his love to others so they can **SEE GOD,** too.

WOW. WOW. WOW.

Do you feel like you have to be someone you're not?

God's love brings freedom to be uniquely you.

14

You can be free to take risks, free to have fun, **and** free to be fearless.

God wants everyone to hear his message of freedom.

15

DO YOU FOLD
under pressure?

YOU CAN DO
HARD THINGS!

you can obey when everything inside you says, "no way," because god's got your back.

He's got the power.

Did you know as a hero
you have a secret weapon?
It's your voice!

your words are POWERFUL!

your words can encourage and bring life to others.

you can use your voice to make a positive change in yourself and others.

Being a hero may sound like a big responsibility!

20

You're not limited by the little you have because God has the power to take your little and make it more than enough.

you can
think big!

God is changing the world with his

LOVE + POWER

and he's using kids to be his heroes!

22

DO YOU want to join this REVOLUTION?

HOPE

LOVE

truth!

23

YOU CAN BE A HERO.

LOVE WINS THE DAY

25

 ## About the book...

You can be a hero was a multi-generation collaboration.

Dreamed, designed and developed by
Becky Olmstead, Karen George,
Meagan Bateman & Camille Paradis.

Together, young and not so old, they
are championing the dream of God for
the next generation and beyond.

For more books by Becky Olmstead,
check out *The Best News Ever*

beckyolmstead.net

CPSIA information can be obtained
at www.ICGtesting.com
Printed in the USA
JSHW010833210521
14980JS00001B/1